P9-CQB-341

Not Quite Ocean

Selected Poems of John Elsberg

COMPILED BY CONNIE ELSBERG

Copyright © 2016 Constance M. Elsberg
First Edition

All rights reserved. No part of this book may be reproduced by
any means, digital or analog, without permission from the publisher,
except for brief excerpts for the purpose of review.

ISBN-10: 0-931181-51-8
ISBN-13: 978-0-931181-51-1

The poems in this collection are gathered from eight of John
Elsberg's books, and nonbook poems were previously published
in print or online at *American Tanka, Broadkill Review, Delmarva
Quarterly, Edgz, Haiku Canada Review, House Organ, Inland*, and
the *Tanka Society of America Newsletter*.

Cover art: Wayne Hogan
Book design by Nita Congress
Printed by Main Street Rag Publishing, Charlotte, NC

Paycock Press
3819 North 13th Street
Arlington, VA 22201
www.gargoylemagazine.com

Not Quite Ocean

ALSO BY JOHN ELSBERG

Cornwall and Other Poems, 1972

Poems: George Cairncross and John Elsberg, 1975

Poems: Lyn Lifshin and John Elsberg, 1978

The Price of Reindeer, 1979

Walking as a Controlled Fall, 1980

The Limey and the Yank, 1981

Home-Style Cooking on Third Avenue, 1982

Torn Nylon Comes with the Night, 1987

10 or Less, 1989

The Affair, 1991

Father Poems, 1993

Offsets, 1994

The Randomness of E, 1995

Family Values, 1996

Broken Poems for Evita, 1997

A Week in the Lake District, 1998

Small Exchange, 1999

Sailor (the father poems), 1999

South Jersey Shore: Poems and Brief Sketches, David Clark and John Elsberg, 2005

Catching the Light: 12 Haiku Sequences, John Elsberg and Eric Greinke, 2009

All This Dark: 24 Tanka Sequences, John Elsberg and Eric Greinke, 2012

To Bogg's readers and contributors
and the many writers with whom John
corresponded over the years—in short, the
community he enjoyed and helped to build.

"The poem refreshes life so that we share,

For a moment, the first idea..."

—Wallace Stevens

Table of Contents

Foreword

John Elsberg was a friend and colleague for over forty years, and I was delighted when asked by Connie if I would write the foreword to this collection.

I have always been a great admirer of John's work and saw how it changed and progressed over the years. My first contact with John was when he was a contributor to *Bogg* magazine from the very early days, either Issue 2 or 3 around 1969. I can no longer recall what the poems were as I no longer have any early copies of the mag, but it would be interesting to see how they would compare with his later work.

I am familiar with many of the poems in this collection having published them in *Bogg* and read them in various other collections of John's work. Others are new to me, but what becomes apparent on reading them is that John was a craftsman, a weaver of words. He spoke with an individual voice outside of any trends or cliques. Some poems are short, almost minimal, but, at the same time, in their imagery encapsulating the whole scene in just a few words.

The three poems "Pastoral," "Collage," and "Virginia in Late August" are all fine examples of John at his best, with their lyrical descriptive content, capturing the mood and essence of the place and time.

I live in a seaside town and John's poem "The Beach" is so evocative of the scene I experience almost every day of my life. Reading the poem is almost like standing on the sea shore itself—not just reading so many words on a page—so vivid is its imagery. No mean achievement for a writer who had spent most of his life in an urban setting.

His poem "Moving On" is about an old van that has been laid up and then restarted with all its inherent problems.

The magnificent phrase "blue smoke of anguish" sums it all up. Then again in the poem "Only in Things," the phrase "the leaf quicksteps across the garden table" gives a beautiful and vivid image.

John was always prepared to experiment, as in the poem "Michelangelo's Dream." It depicts a square graphic block of the one word "Rough," repeated continually to form a diamond pattern in the center, and revealing the word "Abracadabra." No spaces, no punctuation, and it really works.

Another in a totally different mood is "Light," written for the wedding of his son Steve in 1998. The day itself, the young couple, and their future promise are brought to life in a poem of powerful imagery.

What becomes apparent on reading through the collection is that whatever John was writing about, whether it was the urban scene, the countryside, or personal events in his life, the end result is always satisfying in its entirety.

John was a writer in full control of his craft, a wordsmith who never fails to impress.

—George Cairncross
Filey, North Yorkshire
2016

Editor's Note

certainly never expected to put together a collection of John's poems. I thought he would live to be an "old, grizzled poet," as he put it, and would write many more poems and produce his own collections. I wish that were the case, but in his absence I have tried to capture his distinctive voice and to include the range of styles he employed. This is not an effort to collect all of his poems, but to provide a good overview.

John spoke in a variety of tones: ironic, whimsical, funny, childlike, romantic, deeply contented, disillusioned, dark. One can hear such varied influences as Wallace Stevens, William Carolos Williams, Jon Silken, the Beats, and Basho. My favorite poems are those that capture a natural scene or a moment in time in condensed language and striking imagery.

The poems are, roughly, in chronological order, based on publication dates, but it was difficult to date some of the poems, and John often reworked poems which appeared in different versions. There are, however, forms and themes that surface at different points in his writing career, with haiku and tanka appearing relatively late. It will work equally well to follow the progression or just skip through at your leisure and enjoy.

— Connie Elsberg

Ode to Charles Ives

Your movement
was lyrical:

    your ear
    questing for
    the grail contained
    within the white plane of the old
    barn door

    even
when you wriggled your
fingers like a child at me through the bars.

Object Lesson

The little boy
dressed like a man by his
mother, sitting near,
motherlike,
throws crackerjacks
to the pigeons.

They come to him, move
with his every toss,
crackle and jostle and jump
over each other,

a gray mob
going mad in the afternoon.

The boy throws
the pieces as close
as he can
to the one white pigeon,
the one that
almost always
gets squeezed out

(even a little man
can spot a loser).

But after a while
he tires of the game.
"They're greedy," he shouts
to no one in particular,

and then again,
despite his mother's hushing,
They're greedy!"

Pastoral

Here in the woods
far above the house
the fallen trees
are everywhere.

Some sprawl across
the brook, on rocks
scattered
with all the fierce

abandon of spring.
Others
are caught
half-way in the air.

But most lie more simply
on beds of leaves
already slipping
into oil: an almost

comfortable fusion
of decay,
a quiet side
to what passes

as the inner logic
of the seasons—here
where once a boy
came sliding

and short-jumping down
the hillsides as if
nothing else
could stop him

except the water,
that is
always
the bottom line.

Pastoral Fragment

Here in the forest the fallen trees
Have different points of reference.
Some sprawl across the brook, or over
Rocks scattered with the abandon
Of some immemorial fierce flow.
Others are caught in still-living branching.
But most lie more simply on
Beds of leaves already slipping
Into oil: an almost comfortable
Fusion of decay, a quiet side
To this apparently ordinary
Upheaval against the passing grain.

Cornwall

The lantern was a red glow
at the harbor mouth, at the closed
break in the breakwater. Seventeen
foot tides, the old man told us,
had closed it; the implanted wall,
of great wood and iron beams, kept
the water down to twelve, and the village
unflooded. But tonight, after days of rain,
the stars are out. The old houses
round the basin glisten with
a silent sorcery of light
on the dark water, complementing
themselves while rising into steep hills
that layer the next ring. The few boats
ride in an undisturbed randomness,
adding their whiteness to the image
of a womby home. The red danger
is not here—but in the approach, beyond
the stone. Yet the attraction of watching,
in subservience to the glow, is the sense
that this tourist-hiding fishing village
peace is not quite what it seems to be.

Poem on Walking Down an Icy Hill

It was

touch and go!

Ode to Charles Ives #2

Pilgrim, I can
hear you: your movement
as a searching

in the white plane
of an old New England barn door—
in its paint and cracks

and rough grain, in the hewn heart
of simplicity and clear
air—even

when you banged
your cup
like a watchman's warning

in the night, even
when you shifted so abruptly
from the hymns (sweet bye and bye) to trombones,

to percussion, even
when you wriggled your fingers
in a gesture like a child's friendliest greeting

through the bars.

Hospital Room

hospital rainy day dull
gray city streets curtains
like gauze a quiet
splattered down
especially since it's Sunday
lying on my side tired
by papers routine feeling
heavy as if just having made
love to someone I've flattered
without meaning a word
with no way to leave

I would like a crystal
something as fragile and as
promising something
to revolve in my hands perhaps
seeing a sign in the angles
of the glass making more
at least of whatever light
there is trying to catch
Time itself in a moment
of objectified Truth

or hurl it or hurl it

The Clearing

I tell her I feel like a
dragon that has lost
its fire why don't you come
out into the clearing she
asks into the clearing? without my
fire? For the sun
says she to get well to be
slain say I without
anyone's remorse too silly says
she too true say I as
that first wisp of smoke
begins
to rise

The Price of Reindeer

The reindeer
in southern parks
    have gifts the children
hear in rhymes
    still white as snow.

And all the round
of morning eyes
    have gift intentions
of perfect form
    and brightest color,
though hidden in peanuts,
crackerjacks,
    and other good missiles
that go click-clack
    like cowboy trains
into adventure.

The gates are closed at dusk.

And then the sleep
of reindeer fills
    the neat enclosures
like a rolling mist,
like a movement without
    a history,
like the snow on the hills
    in lower Connecticut.

Michelangelo's Dream

```
R O U G H R O U G H R O U G H R O U G H R O U G H
O U G H R O U G H R O U G H R O U G H R O U G H R
U G H R O U G H R O U G A R U G H R O U G H R O U
G H R O U G H R O U G   A B   U G H R O U G H R O U
H R O U G H R O U G H A B R G H R O U G H R O U G
R O U G H R O U G H   A B R A   R O U G H R O U G H
O U G H R O U G H R A B R A C O U G H R O U G H R
U G H R O U G H R   A B R A C A   G H R O U G H R O
G H R O U G H R O A B R A C A D H R O U G H R O U
H R O U G H R O   A B R A C A D A   O U G H R O U G
R O U G H R O U A B R A C A D A B U G H R O U G H
O U G H R O U   A B R A C A D A B R   H R O U G H R
U G H R O U G A B R A C A D A B R A R O U G H R O
G H R O U G H   A B R A C A D A B R   O U G H R O U
H R O U G H R O A B R A C A D A B O U G H R O U G
R O U G H R O U   A B R A C A D A   U G H R O U G H
O U G H R O U G H A B R A C A D U G H R O U G H R
U G H R O U G H R   A B R A C A   G H R O U G H R O
G H R O U G H R O U A B R A C G H R O U G H R O U
H R O U G H R O U G   A B R A   H R O U G H R O U G
R O U G H R O U G H R A B R H R O U G H R O U G H
O U G H R O U G H R O   A B   R O U G H R O U G H R
U G H R O U G H R O U G A R O U G H R O U G H R O
G H R O U G H R O U G H R O U G H R O U G H R O U
H R O U G H R O U G H R O U G H R O U G H R O U G
```

12

Maturity Comes Hard

We are told
even as children
to hold steady

to what we are
to what we come from
to what we own

but circular
reasoning
has misled before.

Undercurrents

In deep winter
the old house surrounds
her with rattles
and drafts and unexpected
settling sounds.

She sits before
a window that overlooks
the snowy fields
and the lake where skaters

add bright colors
to the last light of day.
She cups her baby
to her breasts, letting
the small mouth

pull out her pulse
through the milky branches.
Sad, with fewer hopes
than just a year

or two before, she watches
the skaters go round
in soothing patterns
of movement lost
to her now. They build

a fire near the ice,
a fire to keep
the night for skating,
and as the flames

take hold, she sees
reflected on the banks
the white undercurrents
that sustain her
almost against her will:

snow becoming milk,
wide in soft curves.

Exiles

1.

He peers between the flowered
curtains   the cottage was built
for servants in the 18th
century   the floors slope and the casements
have settled at odd angles
to the street   outside   after midnight
there is only the rain.

2.

He puts down a book and thinks
of Cromwell   deadly
pious Cromwell   who pushed
back the sea to reclaim
the Fens   where churches are now locked
at night against
so much darkness.

3.

Upstairs a woman
is sleeping   she is dreaming
of endless possibilities
of love   she is warm   she is
green   she is in a high
summer's field beneath
an azure sky   and she has never
left the promise of the New
World   that is her only
world   in those memories that still
possess her   and give her
comfort   and give her stillness

in the rain

Cambridge, England

17

Life Histories

we stayed beyond
our first
expectations

we took on
external
forms   roles

materialized
in the
places that

we went to
and in
the night

it became
increasingly
unclear

who benefited
most from
the separation—

our private
selves
or the general

good of the
office
yes   we were

going to be
and became

more serious   more

punctual
more
everything...

but why do
I feel
so alone   here

with you just
across
the room

we ignore the
uneasy
movement

the sadder
turn of
pages   silences

almost tangibly
balloon
the little

boxes of what
we might
have said...

is there really
nothing
left for us

to caress now
except
what we fear

has gone?

The Element of Surprise

(in an English country churchyard)

1.

reading the old

    tombstone twice— "life is long/

        eternity short"

2.

spiked black tombstone

    in Norfolk—   "He killed

        his wife/Pass on"

Junk Ball

A junk ball pitcher doesn't have
a good fastball any more.
Perhaps he never had.

He has to rely on his wits
to get by,
for he knows that grace, like the numbers,

is always on the side of speed.
His litany
is only a pagan incantation

of what works that day,
and the combination
is always shifting:

changeup, sharp- and off-speed curve,
forkball, screwball,
and a brushback off the change

(not more than once
or twice a game)
to keep the batter honest ...

The list, of course, could go on.

But let me simply admit
that I tried them all,
that even in high school my fastball

was too slow for anything
except surprise.
And yet I savored the challenge,

its element of remembered
mystery, as if there was
some perfect pitch,

some constancy of twist and bend
that could yield
a golden summer

from a high-kicked alchemy
of deception and control—
but in relief,

always in relief,
when one could seize upon
that sublime vacuum

left by faster pitchers,
when timing and patience
could be sufficient

to keep even the best
of swingers off their stride,
at least the first time

through the order.
And little changes.
For the threat to any day still remains

the unheard crack of runs,
the game now played
for only slightly different ends.

And when the score begins to mount,
I still catch myself
thinking in junk ball terms,

trying to calculate
that right moment to make my appearance,
and that right time

to turn the ball over.

Mayor Barry

(Found poem, Washington Post*)*

People
who live
in glass houses

shouldn't get stoned.

Letting Go

andishalldanceonthelipofthenightat
theedgeofalongdownhillrunthathasno
bearingstosteerby

forwhenthereisnootherplacewhosepromiseis
dancingthennothingwillrestrain
me

iamwearyoftheefforttobegood
iamwearyofthosewho
woudlcriticizemystumblingasno
dancing

iamwearyoftheefforttobethem

24

Crane in L.A.

are there no connections?

he wrote of Maggie
and God cried
out the apple in the seed
is in the orchard
springing
and the orchard is in the
city beneath
the muddy streets
and the muddy streets are
in the city
beneath the asphalt
sprung

are there no connections?

he put down his pen
and God
cried out again now
nothing's left
in heaven
except these voices
which are
the people who are
the seed whose
memories are so deep they have
to be brought
up like water from a well

are there no connections?

when he fell silent
God was in the streets

Virginia in Late August

There is a softness in Virginia light
in late August the light promises
of the good days of autumn to come
it is the reward for enduring all
that sweltering heat of mid summer
it does not pretend to have dark shadows
it is the light of unwinding of having
a beer on the reclaimed front porch
feet propped on the rail it is
the light that gives a distance to all
those small defeats of the past a softness
that comes from that coolness after mowing
that makes any virtue as easy
as the curl of the bead on the glass at rest

Scrimshaw (Or, Diminishing Returns)

I was bone and blood
bone and
blood I was nothing more
than bone and
blood you ate the
flesh now you have taken the
muscle and blood you
have had your
fill

but you cannot
eat the bone I have kept the
bone I am still my own
sharp angles of
bone I am the living bone I am
my own salvation of
bone I am the
last
of the bone

to be carved

Item

The green ice
that fell—a whole
pound of it—
Into a garden
in Addlestone

(tearing off
a branch of a tree)

when analyzed
was found to be
frozen urine

(released at a high
altitude).

There was little chance
of finding the culprit,
said the police.

(Based loosely on an item in the Guardian*)*

28

Sailor

My father is a sailor. Told me
stories of all places, long
ago, another world, where bright
mornings could be harbors, fast fists
a proud man, and an easy woman
clean, a good laugh, and if not, discarded
like the easiest virtue. Just gone
seventy, and in a white healthy
stride, he writes me a short note
with my mother's busy letter: the household
keeper, as strong as ever in his
uncomfortable lines. And once
I would say he was an *engineer*, marine,
but no longer—he was an oiler, a fireman,
and has remarkable hands to fix
anything, and understands machines
with a perfect visual clarity,
at ease with the gleaming. His was no
better world, a hard life,
but he makes my mother happy, safe
in his gruff smile—and brought
me up at a distance only of what
he really couldn't understand,
wanting me tough, not knowing what
to say to my school mind—saying
study as far as you want, and can get.
Next summer, he writes, come home, I'm
waiting. We'll put a new roof on
together. And to his past, his care,
his silence, I will, with a longing.

(1968)

29

Complexity

1

My father was a sailor.

2

Nearly fifty years between us.

3

Images of his wandering life
suspended like ornaments.

4

Living room is green:
objects just as carefully ordered
as before.

5

Perhaps a generation
had been lost, some intermediate
father, who would throw a ball,
be at that median point,
a balance.

6

I would have told him
that love can keep the bonds
of trust intact despite
the changes, but that

would have violated his sense
of what must be shown more than said.

7

My father was a sailor.

8

In time the distance
that had grown between us
at least became clearer: compounded
of two stubborn wills
and his knowledge that his son,
his only son, was better
at books than with the tools on the wall.

9

The "stuff" of life,
the complexity of father and son,
the promise left
by a long walk on the beach,
talking about the ambiguities inherent
in a sense of self.

10

In grief there are always temptations.

11

Love as the hope
of some mutual resolution.
Loss as the absolute
removal of even the uncertainty
of its fulfillment.

12

My father was a sailor.

The Brook

the water
beneath the ice turns away

from this winter's
unyielding

closeness—

its liquid clauses
have
no tense

this is the moment
between

a season's loss

and the coming
of what
will have

no certain
bounds

this is when
the water

sings

Wetlands

1

My father
is slipping
away

his voice
within my voice
is fading

2

the wind that blows
from the sea
on his house—

now my house—
still carries
the salt

of spawning
and that special
smell

of wetlands mud

3

he is in the reeds
he is in the salty tide
he is with the birds
and with the fish

but he is not with me

One More Time

ten years later
snow down
water as snow
gutters need repair
water as ice
hard ground
no returning now
outline of trees
filling a blank space
outline of trees
so cold
and compact
and quiet
outline of trees—
just waiting
for the spring
waters
just waiting for what
cannot now
be said
outline of trees
as what
lingers after
and beyond that—
beyond water
just the current
of what will be
renewal
just the semblance
of what remains
in me:
his voice

in water

Moving On

Eighteen years later,
his old van:
rust again

but driven every day—

until the heat
this summer

engine box
like a radiator

and so six weeks
in the driveway

and now
all sorts of things
are wrong—

blue smoke
of anguish,

a crick in the steering:

young couple
game

to restore it

A Week in the Lake District

(excerpts from a journal, 1997)

Sunday

arriving   branches brush the sides of the bus

white sails on Windermere   snatches of wool on the trail

Monday

breakfast together in the Hall   loading my backpack

ancient circle of stones   out come the compasses

Tuesday

cairn on top of the fell   we stop to eat a boxed lunch

visiting   the wife of our hiking guide is a doll maker

Wednesday

standing on Hadrian's Wall   echoes of fierce Scotland

in the ruins of a mile fort   a window with a view

Thursday

the cows come up after the sheep   our schedule

Dove Cottage   a fire burning in July

Friday

today we climbed the highest peak   now giddy in a pub

sky still pink at 10 o'clock   more a painter's world

Saturday

a farmer's bright red circles on the sheep   high grazing

last night   hugs and a lesson in croquet as our reward

Light

(for Laura and Steve)

Light is in all the far
corners this day,
light through high windows,
light in eyes,
light in the ease of step and embrace

Light is now
and for the future:
light in two young people
who brighten
this place, this world
for all of us who have come—
come to share in the light,
rekindle our light

Light is in these promises,
theirs and ours

But light, light most of all
is in their love—
let it nurture
all their hopes,
all the living passion of their years

O yes, let it shine.

Taking an Old Dog to the Beach

(for Jenny)

her boy,
running for miles—
   she knew all the routes

checking
each morning—
   her breathing

sugar water
to wash down the pills—
   trusting eyes

purple sweater—
walking through the gaps
   of early spring

she eats
less and less—
   but a hot dog!

taking her
up the block to Nan's—
   the lure of cats' food

two cats,
she knows them—her plate,
   she growls

first signs
of spring—
   her bed on the porch

Tess comes
when we're gone—treats
from her pocket

one day
at a time—
one time at a time

white muzzle.
slow moving—
the young dog licks her

Jenny, Jenny,
such a wild girl—
you still set the pace

she waits for me
to hold her collar
down the steep steps

for the first time,
driving her—

she lies
across my lap—her breathing
becomes my breathing

such tired eyes—
can we go for a walk?
the pack, yes

saying the word:
"beach"—
her ears rise

long ride,
rising to watch—
across the field with us

a house at the beach
that she knows—
checking it out

breezy porch
in early spring—
carried to the sun

the black dog
being walked—
she remembers her bark

for the first time,
driving her—
three blocks to the beach

she finds a good smell—
pees on it,
moves on

walking farther
than we thought—
staying close

she stops
in the sand
and looks, and looks

she makes
the turn when she's ready—
we follow

this way to the car,
she'd rather explore—
can we?

looking back
at the ocean—
one more time

Eight Haiku

power lines
cast long shadows
on the hot asphalt

a beetle lies still
in the shade of one strand

owl watching
from the broken roof
of the old barn

rear-view mirror—
where did all those clouds
come from?

hiking down
the steep trail—
loose stones

driftwood
worn by the sea—
blowing sand

frog chorus—
walking home at night
from the country bar

Distant party
sounds—harvest moon,
white path of stones

Only in Things

the leaf quick-
steps across the
garden table

then nothing, flat,
but momentary—

in the mind
there's a certain wind
already moving

it

Tanka

a slant of light
across the room's
barren wall
the hospital's to and fro
white noise

The Beach

1

I like to go down
        to the beach: the sand, the sun, the acres
                of space in the buoyant
tanning inches... and I like the waves,

        their incessant flapping,
                        like the sound of pages
                in a heavy, unyielding volume
forever closing, especially when it's time to go

                and someone's waiting.

2

The squabbling of the gulls
        adds another side:
                but the standard of spleen
is set so impossibly high that the challenge is seldom

        accepted—instead,
                the children run
                        with all the exuberance
of finding a whole new world purely by chance.

And often I stay
                into the dinner hours,
        when the sun gets mellow
as the wind grows brisker, and then I feel

the moments of the beach
flowing over me,
            the end of the drain,
in touch with the outermost reserves of well-being,

that sail in like the night.

Collage

moon reflecting

on the quiet water   how distant

the other lights

light of a half moon

over the back bay

lone sailboat at anchor

the umbrellas   welding sparks

go first   lifeguards whistling   on the rusting trawler

at the storm   its slack lines

going home   not quite ocean   not quite bay

(Cape May-Lewes ferry)

Tanka

but for the mist
settling in the trees
I could bear
that lonesome sound
cutting through

Slaughter Beach

1.

Slaughter Beach
so much unknown history
in a name

2.

dogs off leash
beyond the dune houses
so much is theirs

3.

clear lines of sight
without regard to season
clear sight

4.

an hour's drive
back to the Midshore woods
sand in our shoes

Three Haiku

after drought

rain finds the leaks

    a cardinal drinking

summer night   smooth lake   a ripple catches fire

looking over
my neighbor's fence
more of the same

When Money Is No Object

summer storm
sleek

boats
narrow slips

now safe
taut

lines
constrained

from turning

slapped

A Haiku Sequence

vanishing snow
and the prodigal wheat
softly
     softly

high corn
in late summer
tasseled steeples

moon rising
big night's calligraphy
on the Bay

the long hours
of farming
sweet carnival time

Tanka

sunmer heat
barn swallows sweeping low
in wide circles
a corner nest on the porch
we now share

In the Wake

driftwood
cradled again the dunes
      color of bone

*

the Snake Brothers play
Temptation on the boardwalk
    slender legs

*

    brushing sand
from my notebook
    no words on the page

*

turquoise running
just off the beach
twilight's soft compassion

*

she sketches at dusk from the dunes   fading lines

*

late summer
dragonflies along the edge
of a wobbly sea

*

sunset over the back bay   a tree turns orange

*

the quickness
of the shell I reach for
outgoing tide

*

going home   not quite ocean   not quite bay

*

everything that we
        leave behind is in the wake
                the gulls keep pace

Island Ice

      watermen
of the Chesapeake
          oyster dreaming

*

clear lines of sight
without regard to season
clear sight

*

swollen creek
the old footbridge billowing
in nuclear foam

*

      a distant creak
of oarlocks
     leaves floating on the skyline

*

dogs off leash
beyond the dune houses
so much is theirs

*

Cherry Lane
to River Road   to Sunset
knowing the way

*

Nor'easter   sand carving the bones of lost sonnets

*

a window seat
and Harry's Readers Salad
writing this

*

passion fruit sorbet
splashed with mango rum
"Island Ice"

*

black woods
beating like a drum
night's calling   calling

Commodities

gold hands
platinum undershirt
uranium   heart
the masters of Wall Street
have been   touched

*

the sly quiet
of a weekday morning
in the suburbs
just this drifting   lullaby
mower   to the grass

*

perfect children
choosing   perfect pumpkins
in early twilight
we still don't know
how deep   the darkness gets

The End of Sleep

the end of sleep
comes   without a ladder
I meant to glaze
the stars   for the sun to fire
but the moon said higher

*

animal
clouds   charging
off the beach
sand-crusted children
stop   to give them names

*

a lone heron
rehearses its stand
at the channel's   edge
a rusting trawler
going home   at sunset

All This Dark

all this dark
stubble   in winter sun
but I know
beyond the next turn
the wheat   is neon green

*

cardinals
stay with us   through
the winter
an oriental bush
that blooms   in fall

*

late geese
across   a rising moon
long trumpets
playing in a royal court
they exit left   on cue

About the Author

August 4, 1945-July 28, 2012

John Elsberg was a poet, reviewer, editor, and historian. He authored over a dozen books and chapbooks of poetry, and his work has been in a number of anthologies. He was the host of open poetry readings at The Writer's Center in Bethesda, Maryland, for almost twenty-five years. He also led various writing workshops, including explorations of experimental poetry with high school students.

In the late 1970s, he was the fiction editor of *Gargoyle*. He was also the editor or poetry editor of several other literary magazines, including *Bogg*, *The Delmarva Review*, and *Delaware Poetry Review*.

As a young man, he taught for the University of Maryland, and then he spent many years as an editor/publisher of history books. His poems appeared in journals such as *Hanging Loose*, *New Orleans Review*, *Lost & Found Times*, *Edgz*, *RAW NerVZ* (Canada), *American Tanka*, and *Lilliput Review*. He lived in Arlington, Virginia, and Henderson, Maryland, with his wife, Connie.